antisocial patience

antisocial patience

David Brazil

Roof Books
New York

ISBN: 978-1-931824-61-3
Library of Congress Control Number: 2015933980

Cover art by Francesca Capone
Alternating Twill, reverse face,
handwoven cotton and mohair, 2014

Author photo by Sara Larsen

State of the Arts NYSCA This book is made possible, in part, by the New York State Council on the Arts with the support of Governor Andrew Cuomo and the New York State Legislature.

Roof Books are distributed by
Small Press Distribution
1341 Seventh Street
Berkeley, CA. 94710-1403
800-869-7553 or spdbooks.org

Roof Books are published by
Segue Foundation
300 Bowery
New York, NY 10012
seguefoundation.com

I wished to make these observations
to keep pious minds from despair,
lest, from feeling it impossible
to divest themselves of the natural feeling of grief,
they might altogether abandon the study of patience.

1.

a gunman in oikos & we
hereby steadily resolve to learn
to pray with which means are at
hand to prose us, blackened
hands with residues of wishes,
residues of what it took to
get us to this point where we are
trying to descry what to do next, this
lighthouse. All flaw in
the text of the rite is a cut
in cloth of sacrifice, smoke
pours out & how I shall make
the way to write in snow
is said by one dead in a dream, to
take on the manner of a very old man,
one who is lived through it, one
who there is no way to say from now
whether or now I'll be. Snow as
an eastern law as a sequence of
nows, that rushes chill thru
every deme, as bright as
attestation so your song wont
want for rigor, poured as it is
from law of the sky thru
form it us you happen to
be on any given day, as it
chances, assuming you are form.

But it is in the time that you
have shape you'll chance to be the
conduit of song. So train thyself to heed. O heed.

desolated ground of we
had suffered song now past its
point of reinstantiation but
remaining in its humming in an
us we recommend the use of
time to tone it, throw
a wrench in laws disbarring
all of our affections so
it's spring ripe epoch for
an aubade sequences of lovers
utter to their others &
coevals, compeers contra
every cop who divvies up the
us into the getters and the gotten,
while we fade therefore into law a
better child of the moment than
our kids of flesh but there is
no end to the saying of the
sutras for the dead so we had
best get started, what anyhow's
the opposite of guilty and how
would we know unless someone
asked us, would mere reflecting
yield a consequence or must I
truly look into your eyes inside

the course of common tasks and
ask? Our history's made of
aggregated snows of our
answers to this question, when
the landlord comes knocking, announcing an increase.

we rust like
ghosts in complete steel, we
rut like mice in crevices & there, occluded,
lay we forth the splendor of
edicts of song. for councils or
the common will cannot amend this
pause which is a part of
prosody, its species, subject to
no renovation but by dint of
wind that shall give speaking to
those ones from whom a speaking ought.
our choice, discalced, therefore to
weld the tune from these veiled facts,
which we must first work up the way to
clutch inside our inadequate pincers,
for I had not been given forms of
any use and therefore went to
study where I could, and
failing that I hoped to dream them,
something we are not meant to confess.
Fuck law. Fuck your juridical
dreams, fuck those
compositions. Fuck fucking also,

fuck the escape that abjures
renunciation of the merely given as
my opening move. For glad and
graceful is the hand of her who
undoes the toilsome nets. The
first name I digged up from the
midden of here when I'd died was hers, now gone out
    among roses.

how orthodox was any longer grace, and
how prepared my heart, to sing the
fittest law that entered in strait
chambers of the day, myself within the
day, the weakest seeming thing of any of
the given objects (and if so seeming's
just one more ruse of the old foe idolatry),
to nathless rise or else to make way for
that force by which you'll rise, that
force dubbed grace, a clearing happens
or we oft recalcitrant make it, to
glean the pure from this wrung mass
still sodden with its wash of song, we
said those words as rhapsodes & we were
not ashamed of the gospel, plucking
elements as metrically set we had good
fate to lay them into *breathless* song,
we the therefore chosen as an instrument of
saying song is here among us should we
choose to reckon with the techne,

with our powers which may obey or
be in mere abeyance, idle as
inactived choice, us
thwarted by their walls,
idle as the silent e's in english. Lonesome as snow.

the pith of hymns will
travel to your ears and
dwell there, doing its
small work as fate majestic
over earth decrees, but
subject to her will we
act within a compass within which
I find myself pent up with you, o
distant lover, one of whom I
lapsing into sleep past midnight dwell
upon like law, like law and light, so
fixed upon my heart's the writing that
you are to me, this worldly script I
seek to read as blood from every place
ascends to greet my instruments, my
means of reckoning with each having-faln-out
thing, the streaks of such I was announcing here
a fatal transit for a worldly thing, having
such time alone to make his *artifice* of thought,
to make a judgment as to right and act upon such judgment,
so that such clouds of blood were never accidents but
only further evidence that every day's the
day for choices, that we sit down to do our work's

imperative and the first stage of work is remembrance.
My means of scripting this mingle with the given
flesh of the day to set a final seal upon this song. Now sing.

2.

in lands of
smoke the ring be
set brought choke points to
the fore of our collected
mindstuff bound to silver &
brought to the temple to
eat a long way gleaming in
its own appearance so phen
omena are yield to the fane a
fold in yuga brough us shoeless to
a yore that trembled twixt its
projection & having been
cancelled forever save in our
hearts, we hum this
collect like a tune, we
reckon up the tally of
our footfall as a mode of
gradualis, sicker
MCs than us went to the
wall forever with no trace,
having abandoned all thought of
fruit, but cloud's kid's today
traces contour of the
impersonal heart, unlikely that
it davens to the law in the
general wreck but look
at the root, it says

breathe after, it
says incline, I am ever
still falling toward you.

i found
upon this barren strand a
loop of words & here
is what I did with them, I
made a sitting place & made
a singing nest, a rhythmic re
frain frail and famished which
I could nathless kinda live in,
till today when flaws in wind told
building it had failed, the
resonators shook your law to
pieces, your law was my houses,
your law settled time & now I'm
cast to outer dark & crying
aloud to listen for the echo, yes,
you had gone down into the sequences
of circles this world was to
find the coldest densest darkest
part you did, the judgments
recrudesced like ooze, you
gulped perception from the
source inverted with its
negativa glow, to live all
life within the mystery of
light and never solve it but

the color shows within the
curve of this here incidence,
some accidental object has to
suffice for members of the
tribe we are, to get us there,
for what else do we got?

if you bright forth what is in you,
what you bright forth will save you,
for father has a prefer for the
terms of light, as human
things are brought to gleam upon
their perishing shore like
memory itself, a temporary
landhold for the earth that we
forget we are, a subtile
doctrine gets its
transference in every generation by
them having ears, for even had he
done a miracle you would have failed
to see it, the eye is not a simple
thing such as you believe it to be, our
grave foe in this epoch (and there
is no other) is the false
immediate, what the name
idolatry warns us against.
But a spirit with the lust a
memory begets went down & got
ensnared in mud, & so here I

am to sing you this lil tune, to
say how it is any rescue transpires, by
means of lustrous song a humming
ladder back to
heaven few shall find it in their
worldly hearts to seize. And many
who have heard the law are like a man
before a mirror.

any urgencies inside
the law have found their
pith in you, who are
their day, their
coming to have been, as
we act in our deeds so it
has been in order that
the scripture dot dot dot,
a task you took on all
unknowing by means of this
instrument your hand, or
your eye as a vector of
seizure, but so intimately shall we
fail each other and ourselves,
and that's the story too, and
time its pavanne, and we
on the ground learning slowly what
is necessity, why
have you brought me to this place where
I'm to die in the dark and

uncomforted and
in my confusions, for
just as he partook so shall ye all,
and likewise tremble there,
in the hour of your
perishment you've spent your
life in thought in flight from but
your flight is not and who
shall deliver, teach
your failing heart to find a pray.

lave the heart in
grammar as an aspic a
gainst tuneless days, contra
want of color & to bring thee
into circuits of the law, a
glowing throne from which the
weltered mother wrought new
passions out of tinctures of the
still bright word, crushed
bugs we insert into the
channels of trade that get the
names a sailing in their
sloops and skiffs to
hit the burning shore of
where this word meets you,
not the same place from
which I am writing, having
gone the road into those

other kingdoms, regions of
the murmuring tribes, who
come to us in dreams to
say what we dont always remember, and
we are shy among them, fearful to
remind them they are dead, our
incurable rudeness follows us
everyplace.

train to heed the
trope of song &
follow any master who
will get you to it better, learn
a word in which is wind to
carry you by dint of measure to a
sea-fed cove in which all tastes are
splayed out by silent trades like
my Phoenician wares, for in your
heart alway the song but to
learn the way to train it out's a
techne it will take this human life
to learn and it has routes that
will deceive us, coy unfoldings going noplace
maybe but to flow, and studied their too, of
measure his languor, for not
in this concealment is our metric hid,
bad times beget bad laws, bad
laws beget bad measures,
but our wedge within this shall be of

song, and song's how long it takes and
what time seems to be inside such taking,
what's the frame we build to stand in &
to be your hosts inside of, where we can
get a mind to think an other place, our
first homes, toward which we're ineluctably / advancing.

3.

glossed the song as
song as a command descend through
defiles of that which
has to be washed according
as the sieve we is, a
sieve of snow reticulated by the
fates who each have names that have
come down to us as prosodies, as
facts, as shapes we ought to find a
manner to transmit, as upon any sunny
day you stroll hither and yon like
the one who's adversarial, about
his job, for you are righteous and
a sinner in the same moment, just as
in that picture by the elder Cranach,
but what did you do, in what manner
did you mutter, was a hand raised
or was it held and what was the context where
in all this transpires, what will you then
utter when led before the deacon of the
signals, there to babble forth each act as
it wove itself into the days you now and
then forgot to note were finite but my
friend they did not at any time
discover ways to be forgetting you, this
is David at his most Augustinian, this
is sitting within scions of a
melody transacting business with the

living and meantime abrading the veil,
I come and go about my father's business you might too.

as brandished perish or a
little chance to say it in the
in-between like living or like
any sanction upon song a board or
strand w/in which pent like
perspication in the plangent signal of
event, recked as strobe of wind begot
a leaflet in the channels of your
wayward heart, a thunder got more
pressured by the eye of Labe that
found its way somehow into this day which
is itself the merest link in what would
have led the that unto the this, the
nearest into the furthest but when
we think that all is infinitely far and
infinitely perishing where is the
vessel into which we ought then to be
depositing our tears, or is there some
second way in which we ought to be wishing,
some other finding, and what is the
strategy by which we'd build ourselves
in such sufficiencies to eat that law,
and find it good, and find it sweet, and
find it just, and find it meet,
and find it meet, and find it meet,
and find it meet, and find it meet.

as song's a node of lambent within
stock & nods to all our surfaces according to
the wind it is from heavens scraped utterly of
what does not accord with justice, so
a wove smoke moves to wound any inside
with the triggers that will go from
stable mute to utterance no actuary can
have gone to name, for day calls forth
its causes and what goes over causes,
speaks in excess, what crudesces out of
rupture in the structure of the name
is where I live when I m I is not
such names as chain me in the human
world, for forgetting is one element of
this our human weakness, for which we
pray Mercy and Mercy it dispenseth, so.
A name is naught but that
thing we will climb, a name is
the still-fervent seizure of
donation of the law, among us
now just as upon the primal day,
for it is no other than that day today,
today, today, today, hoc dies, hoc
dies, hoc dies, do you
know this number, do
you want to be in that number, name
and number, we advance without fear from the ranks of the dead.

The ship
was a wound and we went,
we went forth in the
burning rites, for what
we artificed upon that wreck of
lifeworld was the house, an
articulated strapwork upon which I
hung your picture, or whatever
matter served to make a reminiscence out of you,
for to learn such art as draws the wishes out of our
bodies so recalcitrant with lore is no joke either,
is transmission, relevant
as weaving for it is naught but
just branches of that art,
old art, among
our people, which people, the
people not content to number themselves among the
forgetting, this is their participial song,
these are things that must be washed, this
is the bridge it falls upon our art to build as
delicate as law but fortified by song, by
what you can remember from your days on earth that you'll
pass on to whom, to whoever happens that day to be
taking a collecting at the door to the
perfected spindle of the law, from
which I recollect a song of such surpassing sweetness
it is not for mortal air to bear it,
but I tell you this anecdote to whet your appetite. For law.

Locales arrest
the dust and give it shape, so
shape begets a figure to our
longing that can
find its mirror anyplace,
fashion circles out of
pure aporia go begging
any face for what it's lacking, so
if there is law it is the course of
our going to the road for it, the
road which not at any place
forgives us but which is
called Forgiveness, and
we count the syllables like
mendicants as we go, one two, one
two, no particular sutra will be
the one that saves us but when
considered in the event of their
immaculate aggregate, a collection
we can never see but may be shown,
like the light that is beyond the
light, from which the light that we see
finds its propagation, we're
that light's answer, as pretty much every poet knows.

we answer now
the wishes of

those future selves of us
who are laying forever in graves,
that we now work
while we have light,
for soon comes the night
when no man will work,
nor woman neither.

choke on light,
choke on limit,
choke on the lack but
ask yourself twice :
have you done right ?
have you done acts ?
did you fight the good fight ?
was that shit wack ?
did I fight in
ephesus for this ?
why was I born
between the shit and the piss ?
was paul right ?
if so what then ?
i wonder if i might
see my family again.
everything dies,
that's a fact,
maybe what dies
someday comes back.

And this shall be the matter of my song :
What's just, what's the day,
the song itself and what we want to know,
what it is that's in between us and
what keeps me from myself, the snow,
the city where we live, the
law, the snow, the wall,
all aches we profess by dint of being human things,
but speech itself as an engine of prayer shall
neer be my theme for it acts past my
agency to say it, having beset me and
it wrote my fate into my face so that I
looking at my natural image in a mirror
as in James
should never find a way to fail my
knowing of what is consequent upon that face,
and to act in such dark like as such
fates in objects can give us to go by, when
chance looks like chance instead of god's
actions in the sublunary sphere I go
from place to place, I do my wash, I
pay my rent, a sun of starry heaven saving
the password pass the moon inside my heart of
hearts, that most evacuated place, where
nothing is but this little picture that I made of you,
to help me to remember. Or so I gather.

that's the way the
song finds a path to you.
each law that's needful's written into
form if you can teach your heart the manner of its
reck'ning.
it memorizes days you did not see &
whispers wishes in your fatal ear.
Really I just turn over again the
same abandoned puzzles & I
incise a little hope upon their
intrications, pass 'em on to you.

4.

Good your highness patience.
For abide we here on
tufts of love gone
pink in the weft, a
cancelled epoch within which
we have derived a speech
that's adequate (in its
inadequacy to) the voids
we feel. And having therefore peeled the law
to find at last the inmost core in wants,
We're strand berefted and in company
our voices cannot make a transit of.
This is called today in the
speaking of this landmass, in one
manner of its speaking which
went right to the heart & then
expansed to limits donating
shape as it went, so that if
you find it in yourself to
cease from caring this is
what gave to you the shape of
such possible ceasing.
On this we countersweat, to the
contigent flow of any face
on which we found our histories as transpiration,
any saved region of a laminar epoch, but
where will you bring it, where shall you place it.

with strains of destroyed music
we audit the typical gray
to devise if not a law
then a system of procedures
which aid us in the transit,
without however compelling us in the meantime
to die inside our very living,
a difficult maneuver in their palaces,
where every fairy fruit imposed from
long sonatas feeds the rotting part of us,
to make it top,
so our very score is what will lead us into
forever windowless graves.
But any song splits,
which calls for wit,
to tell the flow from right sacrifices
as though there is a judgment to be
made : there is.
Let ensigns of this gap step forth to utter
their commandments into ceaseless gray :
a holy call resounds below the level of audition at
all times, our true mortal frailty resides in
our forgetfulness, another
gnostic diagram. Take note, and
make sure you write it a place you wont forget.

questions / that dirge
as we compose a
unity of
rupture in these
squandered hearts
the use of any
manner of the day we dwelt in
as a toxin
as a righteous plenitude
as where we met
the tickle I felt while you
talked from about a thousand miles away
as you walked on my grave
as I thought of all the dead
as I left off dreaming of you
so that we can say my heart is
only a node of political fact,
which everyone already knows anyway,
but there's a difference still in knowing and then
acting on the the thing or things you know,
in sitting down to work and in
getting work done.
You make a face because I said a
thing you didnt know you didnt want to hear.
Any day is like that hearing.
Everyone gets to it differently.
What do you think that song means.
The phrases in it reoccur in every surface that I
look to to try to escape it.

Just think :
it's all included.
This Say's Law of the
heart laves any mind with grief for what
this world dont hold : the dead, our
other loves, our justices, any worthy
future we could name, we
get together in a squalid place &
talk about nothing and I
wonder, do you
see me when you sleep,
shall I ask and be answered,
will I meet the means by which I
am at last to be most justified by light,
for light has weight,
for light was weight,
and thus we travel
along the length of this table or
infinitely further, as far as all
the wishes will condemn us when we
close our eyes and cling to every
sign of siren in her weight, this
world a woe that stuck like a bur to
the westward person, gone without plan
to where the sun dies and we
as is right feed him horses,
the swiftest beast to feed the swiftest star.

To go outside the way
this version of the world can know a thing
is tactics of my song confronting grey
as consequence of deathless measure
as antinomy for any spirit that
resurges in the boneyard to take up
a lopped region of the holy epoch you
cant fracture with your epicycles, so
we're still athrash within the same
complex of intricates spikes, as
I certainly dont have to tell you my
coreligionist. Let this letter be
a warning that we must not conform
ourselves to this world's
ways, I say this to move you to
shame, to a picture in your
esemplastic faculty that
fountain forming borders
inbetween facticity and the
thing I've been trying to tell you about.

here below sound
is conditioned so we
weave a discourse that
will give us signposts toward
the holy depot, answers
which insist themselves upon us despite

everything but dont have place amidst
administrative cutbacks in the very
possibility, a choked
flow of air's the way you make
this foreign sound soon to become
your name in the course of the
overturning which is
trembling at the veil of
onset's appearance, this
is what theophany looks like,
tell me what theophany looks like.

The grace that lets
the aspirant obtain
a thing by means of struggle
is what we analyze down to the
laws of song, if we know laws
to design tendencies, a
hope for movement toward a
picture of a justice that cannot find
its own delimitation save in
inward folds from which it
moves to cut its shape in time
as sequences that we'll donate
our mite to, so it rains, force
and all forms and us as the
pictures or engines of such
providence we designate according to
the day of words, the ones we learned ,

what species of the finitudes befell us &
the manner of our dreaming there.
You go places but
do you come back.

hunting by force
the earth of resurrection
we sing so
thus clad in gold stiff gold,
the folds of imperial pomp which
ensnare all of us in gaudy fates of our
righteous share of the perfected number of the saints,
for saint thou art now answer the call,
for saint thou art my friend,
for saint thou art and lacking right to flee you shall
be made the thing you do not wish whether or not you wish it,
they say the learner suffers,
they say the hour was a banker's daughter,
they say I am a killer and they are not wrong for
all of what is worst in man has come to dwell in me,
therefore I study how to pray,
therefore this splintered wretched western song.

the angel's name who'll
sound the

resurrection trump
is nowhere found in
holy books, we
must resort to
speech and rumor, desp'rate
Fame that rides advance
of any host and
builds the law of
names out of
raw air inmixed with
wishes, fancies, lusts and hates,
all of what we must at last make answer for,
the litanies of negative confessions
for which we must in advance have
filtered out that filthy blood
in which we bathed, of which we were.

They threw lots,
for cloth, for the
wife, for the song,
for any virtue whatsoever,
in order that the scripture be fulfilled.

5.

We are buried in ourselves like
    lovers' names, like
   Socrates emitting
time in the form of his death, the
     series of the sequences we owe.
As for your and your friends,
  all caught up on the getting of
wealth, recall the pericope of
      the adulteress, o
  wait, that's me, that's
on me, I am one caught wearing
    that robe, opacity on which
I'd counted for my venal
    guile's failed, behold
   here I stand, with my
wet head and bloodied hand.

And when that you had trod the trace
   Make trade with wits for hearts that equal
            And natural face beheld in glass this morning,

As though the morning were any other day
than that of judgment. How then tread & strike,
o inmate of the fate, the fire,
lavish to thine own appointed
comforts like a grave. The table's laid.
The beasts enact their circuits and a
wedge called distance's drave between yourself and
any worldly consolation. Loss it is to
seek thy nectar here, the earth that clots
the mouth of the dead, the snow on the wire
bleeding out his static as
ruined formal garment of the song,
but train your ear and this alone suffices as the clew
to lift thyself to ether and surpass
the wat'ry sphere of the moon,
greenish white and lilac.

The past tense of seeing is seed,
but if the seed not die,
in color as well as in light,
our corpse is washed away by the flood.
But let thy name be buried in my heart,
in this erotic trope of smoke that is
a smouldered bed or work of earth we make forsake to
make a ladder of our passions, how,
for say that we have heeded song,
much heeded, seen
in song our law of recall and a
governance at last to the last things of

gall and the sceptre, im-
mutable blood, the cords
that always will have tied us to the fatal acts that
time's a stage for, so, we
stand in company and audit birds and
human speech, upon this strand that
waves of light and darkness lap, I
said to you what's vanished now
into the emblem of its saying, my
armourer was Eros, my
errors are my own and he shall judge.

A second petition ratifies chance,
so those who seek for cause'll have all their craws stuffed
with hateful laws of needed fact, just 'cos
that's how world-spirit wants it (is what
they'll say to themselves)(NB. spirit's pronounced
"spurt" to keep it
monosyllable)(cue
laugh of Hobbes) to whom a
pact without a sword be-
neath the paper's merely words,
for were all men at liberty,
in prosody or otherwise, we'd
be xxxxxxxxxxx xx hard pressed to
say what that was, a
ballad or a
rent-strike or
the shedding of which fetters,

which now-baroquened objects of the mind made
          dire under epistemic laws ?
"Your song, what does it know ?"

Having sieved the portion for a gospel let
          these fates be known : a word worked
by a human hand not mind is reft from earth
& washed and left to gleam for our reflection,
          so counter to the current law is it that in its
saturation as a moveless tell it has
incited dreaming in these restless kin of age.
To say this is as much as is to say that history still
flows invisibly out the struck rock to threaten
to wash us spies in laving flood, for so I reason
out of the scriptures, the land is stones and
          we have deserved it.

But hear down to the law,
  that sovran tone in things,
    which even if it be the gap by which
    things come to be articulate, that
    freedom inside which we perish of our flaws,
     we still then will have known the thing it was and
      used our wit to honor it, impossibly, this
way that it appears in our own most contradicted hearts,

dying here today of their errors and causes, of
their eyes for days, of all that I could not find the way
to bring to light, to bring to pass, to ask or to confess.
Let doctors say : such gaps light only crosses.

Some men have dubbed it Ariadne's tear,
which seen in the night sky imparteth awe.
My crown is made of grosser stuff than this :
Coarse grasses and impostures of the face.
A chilling woe hath struck me to the verge,
So I may say I am no more a man,
But what man is when he comes to the pass
At which, imperilled, he's to be unmade.
A son of starry heaven in the flesh
Drawn by his lust into the turbid pool
Must strive to recall what it was he meant
To do by being born upon the earth.
There was a thing to find : so set your course
Away from griefs, and toward that holy thing.

6.

For earth had sworn to gobble him
who was most lovely of the jews,
with hair as long as mine is now,
descended from the ranks of priests.
There is no grave, there is no hell
enough to still the speech I've got,
for in my numbers are such men
as claim descent from righteous names.
Did we come to the wilds to die,
struck down by plagues or burnt by fire?
If not then let us gather now
and strike down him who gives us law.
For every man is holy now
Say all us insurrectionists.

Did I not tell thee
that thou couldst not
have patience with me, who
hath drunk from waters of the

confluence, whose name goes unwritten in
any holy book, whom none
but satan
could make you forget?

naked to love's own sword
or stripped by your will, the
case of a room closed to all but
your own mind (if it's yours) as
you recline into soft down of the
long aftermath, a vowel tone consoles you then like wakes as
landmarks in
the stutter, graphic testaments to
progress of your souls' and souls' companions, but
if you are found tortious woe's like
to be your portion, it will take
three hundred donkeys just to bear the keys
to the vaults which hold the treasure of sorrow
from which you'll be fed. The
lore of the fed, the
grief of the green law, look to the fit measures via which
the soul's consoled and dandled on the passing
programs. What obtains and what acquits,
to render up what self as student of it,
in the sense of I gave all according as I knew to give,
a question in the footnotes of the law.

Measuring thy justice by our mutation, so,
that I have traded houses is a moral fact,
these coasts the strands of discipline that
overcomes my right to will, in which travail
I will have paid the debt to know thy way & heed it thus,
for so in works we find our peace by working only,
thinking is a thing that's not the same as starting,
for in starting we remember what it was that we forgot,
our basic frailty, with memory the veil grace wears
on any given day, and even in the midst of living this we
are forgetting, as if the world called for a proof in
supplement, but let me sit and think a while about this, let
me look through my books, let me clear a shelf of time to
say the law as it chose me to effloresce, a granting that
I could not know to want before it hits me like annunciation.

and they died and became like the soil
and their mouths were stopped up with the law
and this is the name of the end of their line
and this is the terror they beheld in the dawn of the judgment
and this is how they joined themselves to things beyond the finite
and this is how the scriptures were fulfilled
and this is the color of the garments they were laid in
and this the tongue they spoke when they spoke last
and this the form of sentences laid down
and this the grief and wailing when they saw
and this the gestures that grew up among them

and this the seed of war within their hearts
and this the face they could not show for shame was in them
this the station down to which they'd fallen
this the great forgetting that they ate of
this the crime they had committed
this the rite they had neglected
and this and this and this and this and
this and this and this and this
and this this this this this this this
these were the ways he came to dwell among them.

clad in dirt my dads are launched
into empyreans that blossom under every law we tell to
survive days,
answering our texts with vatic gaps in which we'd scry if
we had wits sufficient, but, there's our fucked epoch
with which to reckon, dispensing its
laminar paste across the surfaces of love it made a
math of, so we homunculi of its
divides are set to act it out in what it cannot reconcile also
what it lacks, what it's forgot, that trench o'er which
we've taken to economize, to figure out what
we ought to read next. Here's
a song, where's the
music, what's the
score, what's the date. Append here
a tiny glyph that reads grief as
what destroys and also somehow
keeps us walking, where.

to give thanks that we rise again from death and live
for be we song, we are its diagram of graces

as a lattice of the grades we have ascended
or in progressive process of ascent,

self similar and with deceptions of the earth so that
if we remain unmindful of the spirit's facts,

we'll be beguiled into dreaming there's no movement
of the mind to things that are its suns,

for only gathered from the world's opacities,
where our love's infinites could find a pledge of rest,

those rhythmic stops have wrote a script we run to read,
we wrote it and then wrote and read it while we ran,

these being traces of those elements that saying
only scrapes the edges of, so you get it under your nails,

then walk back slowly into town and wonder what the way
    will bee
to say your seeing to those whoevers you'll be chancing on.

after a wreck, say,
women, your song, who
as ensemble are traduced and fucked, and so
become the public wound, for
we all sup on portions we disown,
and devils come with brothers to the
unswept houses : this denunciation then
to brothers who my brothers have the
ears to hear the echo of their private facts
and griefs and woes and crimes and crimes and crimes and
what is woman within you you've wounded, what
plaint would you cry to such a
region within you you'll surely have to pay a debt to,
for care shall change her visage then to that of the
actual judge,
pursuing each such trace, so be the woman now who sings
thy orison and dirge, o
wrapped in your cerement, wrapped in your shroud,
your body rinsed at last like a wedding by paid strangers,
a painting by Courbet.

I live within tone,
and steep is the rent.
The creation groans,
but the message is sent.

7.

Sometimes a man knows
a place determinate,
within the
compasse thereof he is to seek; and then
his thoughts
run over all the parts thereof,
in the same manner, as one
would sweep a room, to find a jewell;
or as a Spaniel ranges the field, till he find a sent;
or as a man should run
over the Alphabet, to start a rime.

beauty is an endighter,
sets the path on you & rove you
rove along the strait or strand old son,
basking in the any-day-now character of
what this form of being is, a
splinter in the fact of mind to
find itself adjusted in the turbid wake of
having clutched the dirt in lust, that
echo just goes on forever, till all resume their
prior state at the start of the circle saith
Origen, still not of the canon for this crime the

thought of a universal redemption, we say it
a po ka ta sta sis
say it with me now
a po ka ta sta sis
you
gotta stay true to your school.

The law will say
there are twelve feasts
of inchanted water, so
you confess your name to
every paper ever after, just as though the
sequence itself was not a remembrance
itself to be forgotten in the fulness of
effulgence, when a release from
bondage these are only figures for shall
blot it out forever, add not
to thy burden by the
heaping of a chain, there
was one whose keys to
treasurehouses were themselves a
burden so he staggered
juiceless in the desert and then
sank to hell alive. The name might
forgive but the law shall never do so,
not three times nor four.

In the days when you devoured the dead,
in the days of the general strike,
in the days of the great question,
in the days of our houses,
in the days when I fed you,
in the days of the new model,
in the days of the tent of the meeting,
in the days in which this song was written,
in the days after the end of days but before the end of the end,
in the days of syntax,
in the days of the prehistory,
in the days of vast forgetfulness,
in the days of bad prosody,
in the days of rust and rust and splinters and rust,
in the days of no money for groceries for everyone but champagne
for some,
in the days of the continent of law that stretched out to the
visible horizon,
in the days of the discovery of the possibility of the relentless long
line of this saying as adequate to social fact,
in the days when something new was truly being born,
in the days when I was upon the earth and saying this to you,
in the days when I planted the trees under whose shade you
are now reclining in order to read this letter that I wrote you,
in the days of the prehistory,
in the days when all this was necessary,
that is when I stood waiting dreaming the possibility of you.

this honor of lending the entrails
knitted as a signal fact to
new law that unfolds as immanence from this
remains unthought inside the
echo we need

these lent entrails
knitted a fact
from folded law
indwelt as thought's
echo we require.

what breaks sleaves'
robust work which
answers smoke a
taken match or
dare against prevailing
tales bewraying nothing
being something's substance
a depleted field
we're walking on
to settle bets
laid someplace else.

Truly
wedded to this circle, I
can dream of viaducts but not proceed to them, so that
in the midst of great expanses of this feast of the forgetfulness it
falls to me to recall any tricks of soteriology I might
have stumbled on for in the winsome light any
one might well forget that so soon comes
the night in which no man can work.
But will we be forgiven for
forgetting's not a thing I
claim to know.
To know.

For with any prop I
knit the web from which
the mirrors hang, according to which means mind
comes to recollect itself, its
limbs in the wild of the thorn.
He places and he dwelt in placing, fixed
by law of the set, and
having placed, the master holds.
You go forth smelling of such smoke,
you go down the road and whistle the tune.

Amnesty is total for the askers only.

8.

Look no further for the chain.
Looped gyves, an
anodyne bled out the spectral day,
so grey so summery the
paste of time was smeared on you,
and what's the upshot ? Your
        fat gleams in the pit you're
full of all uncleanness they
oughta writa book about the ways to scrub off
what you were, they
did, but which one is it, I know I
got it around here someplace.

From thought to thought, from hill to hill love doth me lead.
Clean contrary from restful life these common paths I tread.

Sing the
hymn of the
king of

hell you
stand upon his
turf and talk
his speech he's
operant right
now & standing
in your path as
unseen adversary
working to strand you
to string you up by your own guts.

But I have told thee
by my works my
faulty works the way
to husband this my
lady soul

chance carved waves,
chance made graves.

We / Can learn our names from our mouths

And thinking on the sword thus dubbed
What*I*Will*Risk*For*You there's
the grave always yawning to
spoil our companionship, like
a cop showing up at the party, my
brother I have loved you but
who goes down on who is still the question till
we solve this regume of physical equality,
it's dire, now, this
question, as dire as night when it sets and you know what that
means for a change, having
grown old beneath its dominations,
its oppresions, each object donning at
last its fatal contours which
leads you to read each word out loud as it may be
the omen you've been waiting all your life for,
the ribbon on the gift always before you that
you never got to open, the
tune
you just cant seem to remember,
coming up as a cracker in a casket.

a monogram
in new subsistences
cuts cross to
render doctrine
apostolic so
we sift among the middens for
that which dieth not

The doctrine of the symbol.

The symbol comes to us out of the mouths of the death.
It is the work of those in the grave to weave it.
This is like Penelope waiting for Odysseus.
He is always of course going to come home.
This is narrative.
We'd be disappointed otherwise.
In the same way we will always be going to find the dead.
We'll be the youngest in their number, some day soon.
So the symbol is a sort of echo.
Echo loved us but could only say the last part back.
When the dead find something in us to resonate off of,
that's how they do this work.
This is the original theory of music, as a science of
the passions.
Of our bondage to the passage.
The dead are fortunate because they're quieted, though
often very
bored out there in orbit round the moon.
Anything got by us in this trough is an attempt at metrical help.
There's no doubt but that the bond of flesh has made
us obstinate.
But having sifted up from the woe a grain of remembrance,
temples can be made in any place, to
aid us through the strait.
I'm not the first one to have noticed this,
but you have to look hard amidst all the rubbishes.

"I bathe in the waves of the trace."
I too act within the trade, will be
of its articles, hereby consent to
link in augenblick, a
moment made of this attendance.

The king, they say lies
      raging in a Fit;
Which does no cure but sacred tunes admit;

 and fire, for
  the walls, for
  judgment, days on days of
    immaculate grey undisturbed grey of
    trade,
 the trace of this traffic ommitted from a
  pure panoply of the
  textile wed, the
 course of cash through it as
  profane grace you
 get you dont you
made the grade you
  died in a hole till the
  greyhound come, the

Qwat hast thu don, dawn Water.
sin saterdai at non ?
Thu holdest nowt a note. x
by God ! in riht ton.

Dawn Water strode upon the break
With claws full of permission
He took no more than he could take
In hopes of a remission

His clothes they were of cloth of gold
Though tattered in the wearing
And neither young and neither old
And of but middle hearing.

Born of the east he went the west
In hopes of that worth hoping
But this time's guest like many of the best
Spends all his best time coping.

Ballads are best for heroes blest
And not for men of middle station
But who rests breasts midst the worst and the best
Hears the whole diapason.

as splayed to
visitation
by a grammar
any day now
having name agleam in his paws like
the prophetic instruments, I
crave the law, I
made a grave of my remembrances and
you were there, and you, and you.
The taco truck
dont come this way no more, now we're
in the outer dark, be-
yond appeal.

9.

His thumb is on the
beam of this here speech commune,
rendered clear by wit as feather is,
so you'll get to adjournment safe and clear,
the words will have been said so that
you can go back to your cell with one lite heart,
but me, I cant get clean, the
soap's too dear and I
cant cash the stamps,
I could not live on your wages while
the day flings up endless birds out of its bodies giving
their sermons on a production and meantime here's any one
    of us
trying to reckon the incarnation or our
crumb of it, communicant, in any case,
and crying for the paraclete someplace in
low orbit, in another time zone.
Some say that the soul has parts.

Just totally useless
ridiculous
disgusting fucking garbage.
Unsublatable under any
formal manifold and nathless

here, in fold of any saying,
saying that was his, where
his is wherever sub
specie aeternatis,
grim hub of the glesh having acting
in the channel of an antique law,
which said :

Clumped seed chafed the law
against his time, a prosody
within itself went double,
found a map of how it was to be in any room &
dwelt there, like a light was in a niche like
talk could redeem any damaged vestment of
a how it might have been before you was, the
struggles you had met as this world's work was
smoke, was song, by dint of the act, you
took some really thorough notes they
found one reader, we're lucky sure if we
even get one reader. What
were you doing before this today, what
are you going to be doing later ?

like the eyes of the heart
gone to paste in the strut,

a civic law of dissolution promulgated itself in tender sinews
otherwise than
you intended leading to a consequence where you were
dead and looking on at once, beneath the shade of
any several soung like you could words like
words was young or song or words were the beyond that
wanted to get here by means of your fingers they are the
dead and in your knucklebones and forcing and within that
ink their pleas perhaps or observations maybe to the sorrowful to
know their own condition as a piece of hymnody, de-
parting from the cantus firmus like a book you just cannot get into,
but what the fuck is going on with those upstairs neighbors, what
are they moving around up there, is
rigorously closed to any knowing but by a chance intervention like
they need your help to catch a mouse or
you become friends.
Mouse is the same word in Hittite, we
been coughing up a facet of the law for flickers of the moon, for
an attunement, as
the soul is known as a thing that can count.

For by patience will we
have our souls, did that
song know it was to be a
prophecy in the citation, so
fulfillment is in nature of
some written that it may
come to don the glowing raiment,
white in the fields to see your co-wreckers,

an ambient bleed as histoire sleeps
from the small into the capital haitch, a
fact in any heart including yours according to the
    goddess chance,
that we propitiate with texts and observations, lineaments
    and cakes,
coarse mottos of the mainline and dactyls sore from plaiting
    gifts to
who, to
chance, to you in her
moieties,
on whom the doxa falls like
touches, who are those for whom a name is not.
Sing sang sung is how you show
ablaut, sing is a
verb, Sing Sing is a prison, then
is the world one, a
sort of ergasterion, a
workhouse, Schopenhauer wrote, but
what is the work, l-
earning the work is the work.

And if with god thou time thy hearty song
so proximate the step that pent has lauds,
an Anselme of the trewe has cruelly flawed
a fledgling law of power born in you.
But if thou scoop thy juster foil,
a cancelled gist is yours to renovate

for errand wilder poisons shall you choke
who over naught is made a potentate.

Love, to give law unto his subject hearts
hath wove a song is made of days
and all that you recall, and every art
and harm is laid upon you in your ways.
That you stroke off to old time fancies now
is a fact redoundeth to you woe
for each bleached bleeding fact therefore incized
is but more evidence to one who'll know.
A song is any answer that you gie
which with the burden of a burden shines
and the singing one shall surely live
to tread amid the Rocky columbine.

The author of this psalm is far from Jerusalem.

Will you remember to pay the debt ?

Will you remember to pay the debt ?

Will you remember to pay the debt ?

Will you remember to pay the debt ?

Will you remember to pay the debt ?

Will you remember to pay the debt ?

Will you remember to pay the debt ?

Will you remember to pay the debt ?

And when you sell,
be sure to get my price.

Two years sober,
two years dead,
two months hobbled,
one day fed.

Living on virtue
from check to check
I love you
a bushel and a peck.

For even a man
whose father was poor

has need of a room,
to shut its door.

I was born ;
I was fed ;
I was housed ;
I'll be dead.

Give your thanks
while you have breath,
For you too count,
in the tally of death.

Whatever your face
whatever your rank
the work of this world's
to think and to thank.

10.

The treaty's ratified.
For we have not scope
of boundless time to work these acts,
but without bars we're not & therefore
bent, we sketch the promo packet of these deeds
that shall come after, so I rode
into a space that was prepared
for ought that I might issue w/
my hands as agents, called it
"freedom" & was
sung into the law at just sung point
that it's conjunct with history, so that
stars dove into my cradle &
fed me the milk of their circumference,
in every likewise day of life I've strained
to grasp the whey of that which neighbors time,
implacable as bulkheads which the wreck
shall surely and forever later mingle,
making fuck of all our hapless habs at tense,
saying surely that was then and this is now,
both of them naught but scrims for the presence.

Code.

The milk of code.
A digest of the laws, which is
hewn at last into the tree,
the very tree thru which it coursed,
the pro
hibition judgment and the ransom each
written like math in the facts of my hands.

A
song to wake
my own self up.
The disputation twixt
a sinner and his soule
hath twist the gripes upon this fact,
our soul's cast in
to bodies where it finds
such dross as number, time.
But on this time we sketch the map of
any thinking that shall at last save us,
having been in it unfolded out of most uncordial pith to
know a law from garnered factors,
garlands of the pole of this how
ever brief, him
that is righteous, let
him be righteous still, the
frostbite starts in five minutes.

2.

Who will ascend, must be undressed,
and bound by coils of the earthly wants,
will trace a spire of opacities to chain
the earth to heaven, fucking up the airspace,
clotting all our transits to the gracelands with
the filth of their cupidities, and so
while still on earth we settle to the fervent and
the subtle work of burning

We think the
dirt. We
transit it, and
never are we closer than
when clutching our own
seed or our own
blood, the proper that
in moments has
evaporated into nothing that
this earthly substance always
bound to be shall always show in time,
the very wind instructs us,

show your fetters so's
to exercise the worldly wit to
shuck 'em, duck
and move.

Hist, the very form of song's
a coil binding you to
pictures of the world that you cant get to,
access cometh but by grace so pray &
shrive & build your domicile out of
aspiration going unashamed amidst an
earth consigned to the fire. Find
the ground covert with pearly grain.

For you were given this to dream,
and not by chance, but bound
by recall to a wish and knowing that
therefore not to be attained but finding art
with which to make that wish transfigured, so
that what was past in time becomes a future
into which we're walking, lightened by the
cure of grief of having lost a thing forever by
knowing it is before us, which is the same as to profess we
do not know what thing is time, it comes to us in garments.

I see the swords & spears of futurity, all
that befalls this corpus glossed to give
a matter to its inward Genius, grown
impersonal in late light of this crack'd episteme,
seizing what in fortune comes to make a fact beheld transmissible,
so you, a term of this equation, eat also at this fatal table, are
not absent from its invitations, but
the ones who fall to feasting and forget by
dint of the sauce of the strong drugs of the host, what
plea shall they utter when the great conflagration commences and
they haste to find
the portals are bolted
the portals are bolted

Forasmuch as we the
lame communicants have tread
the road of beauty laying in
the light that filters down into the
gap obtaining between
mercy and the justifier, so
have grabbed up little flickers of
an evidence that comes to rest in us &
makes therein an irritation that prompts
the motions of the soul grown so long dormant in
static desuetudes our upbringing called for.

We know we've a soul because we have terrors.
That's what it was like to have been an actor.

Death is strong, death is the race.

To take you devils have a thousand methods
Method is today the road on which you walk
Tomorrow you'll see all this trash was spirit.

Any poet worth her salt talks to the dead
By means of her own soul which undoes the walls
Placed on gross sense as payment for our errors.

You might have learned by life on earth to fuck it,
To see the two heavens as a pathless grace,
And to punch your mortal clock and eat nice meals.

To you this song in tercets proclaims error,
Working out from time its inmost contrition
Failing as we fail but saying its failing.

Bound to time by song and law this flesh seeks measure,
drawing up from memory whatever will advance it,
erring by not owning that it knows such memory is double,
draws it down or lifts it up as it intends by its relation,
for was such dreaming turbid and of earthly wishes it declines,
but what you loved here is transfigured into light which
link by link delivers you unto the canopy of stars the
meetingplace where you have done the work to forsake you.

11.

the wind is infinite
  my predicate
  my predicate

Bethink thyself of the Pearl

Any room could hold a penitent, it's
time, a shape of the grace on descent
can hold you captive by a picture of
as-though-it-is-the-present,
fatal lie you gulped o grandee heed
delete the dazzle of the sensible & dwell in
palaces of such withdrawl, it's
maybe something somewhat less than
fun you used to have but what's
fun anyhow we're
here to learn a thing I reckon (said
to his own restless lady soul) nos-
talgia for samsara is bullshit but
not jerking off's still a hassle.

to unity with light &
keep it there, so
say then am I free &
at what time, what's
this concept born from what
survives it where
do you think we're going &
how do you act as a
consequence you
dont get away with not
choosing. For
birth is crisis.

I got up to the
palm I siezed the
fruit thereof, it
scorched my partial
gleanings of the law till
like a glowing mass I was
withdrawn to leave a
trace of light upon the
manifold a sign perhaps to
you who sit there reading this,
for what was worked on me is

like to find its work on you,
a gladness that you bore, some
burden that you dragged, but we
like lilies of the resurrection or
like
lilacs

We ask the light.
We ask the death.
We ask our song.
We ask thy roads.
We ask to know thy ways.
We ask the cop.
We ask the chosen few.
We inquire of the book,
we ask for different options, we
ask for an adjustment, we
ask of you for why has this been done,
we ask the glass to count our age, we
ask of our own eye, we
ask a friend to tell us what was up with her, we
ask what's wrong, we
ask the internet we
ask the loveliest blue we
ask the oracle who is
the wisest man in Greece we
ask the president we ask our
building manager about the plumbing we
ask language itself we

ask for a raise we
get together and we ask for it all to be over or
this version of it anyhow we
ask Hegel when we're stuck in Switzerland we
ask mom we ask dad we ask your father we
ask what's going on we ask did you hear we
ask what's your problem we ask did you like that we
ask can you help me we ask do you think I am lovely

12.

David the king
was greatly grieved
and he went to his chamber his chamber and wept
and as he went, he wept and said

O MY SON

O MY SON

would to god I had died
would to god I had died
would to god I had died for thee
Absalom my son my son

and as he went
he wept and said

O MY SON

O MY SON

would to god I had died
would to god I had died
would to god I had died for thee
O absalom my son my son

you hold it, feel
the human noise, a
crackle of the been, en-
teric brain, it all
repeats in pattern so I
clutch & am clutched in return am thin-
king what's the price
I have to pay to get out of
going through all these things twice

I was dead.
They buried me.
  They put me under
the sycomore tree.

I was ashes,
I was a thing,
I was coming before
  the throne of my king.

  All mortal things
  had had their day,
  and now it was time
for me to pay.

There is a judgment,
there is a scale,
if you are as I was,
then you will fail.

I was once
as you now are ;
you'll be like me,
the day's not far.

Prepare yourself
as best you may ;
there are no secrets
on that day.

Wretched is the cursed land
consumed rather than watered by
these three rivers of fire :
libido sentiendi, libido sciendi, li-
bido dominandi.

In writing these melancholy notices to you, I have taken especial notice of the vanity of human works, seeing man as though it were from vantage of a certain eternity, where what he accomplished is as miniscule as those animals seen beneath the lens of a microscope, but where contrariwise his sins, the most intimate betrayals of those closest to him, and as well himself, and not least GOD, and which are so oft shrugged off as of no consequence, and petty in themselves (but they are not petty when considered as betrayals!) ; these, in light of that same eternity, expand to seem as though they were the emblems of his absolute, his helpless depravity, and inability to surmount the devil ceaselessly beside him, to vex him to do mischief. For he has had his whole life to do good, and instead he did its reverse; saying first that it was of no consequence, and second, if that lie was not sufficient accomplice to his self-love, which excuses everything, that certainly the ill deed was well hid. Woe, however, to the malefactor. For sin is of consequence, and nothing whatsoever shall be hid.

DESERT FOR ALL OF MUSIC TO TAKE PLACE,

It's just another way of saying form, if
I could but touch the hem
of any eventual daydream of you I could tell her
but the facts conspire otherwise to
shape an everyday nothing which
I inhabit just as though it were life,
second or third coffee, water like
the liner notes just a xerox of the
'daily life of the artist' meantime shuffling
towards a compromised ontology
made of deleted dollar signs, the ownmost you were
aiming for is "sober and industrious"

and getting pickier by the minute, these
                    pants need a wash and your
wedding invite's in the left front pocket, no
                    right, remember the last time we fucked,
me neither, ever since I got all my shit right with god
                    there's just less good gossip, I even
deleted my secret naughty email account so there's no
                    hope of reaching me there any longer, I'm
just a different person, I say the lord's prayer with
                    emphasis on evil, for the
law of other members works in me, time is that pavanne
upon which
                    we enact betrayals and can you imagine
standing in the afterlife, looking at the scorecard? "None
                    of us getting out of this thing looking good"
said a guy to my dad but they're all
                    dead in here that's why we have to
innovate in form just add it up just add it up just add it up, just add
it up

Go immediately to the worst place imaginable and linger there awhile writing out of what you see. If it is the dead people go to the dead people and say their names out loud like they were segments of the rosary. (June, Robby, John.) If it is god and you dont want to pray or know how to pray start praying, just start speaking like god was someone else in the room that you just dont happen to be able to see, don't worry, you're smart enough to be able to innovate the appropriate form as your god. If it's your crimes make a list, consider them in your mind, turn them over in the hands of your mind like they are something that you found in the street and are considering whether or not to take home. Just remember that you already took them home, they are just as much a part of you as anything you ever did that you are proud of. They are pride's shadow. If it's sex ask why you want what you want and how much it structures you, ask where your wounds came from and who gave them to you and how you passed them on as wounds to others and whether or not it is possible to stop. If it is the disasters of the world or history consider them and consider also their effects on you. Consider is to go with the stars. Consider is related to desire. What draws you out of yourself, whether love or affliction, is a meridian that will take you just exactly where you need to go. Remember that you cannot imagine what it has taken for me to draw this page out of myself, even what it has taken to draw out of myself the line that I am still in the process of bringing to its ineluctable completion which I will defer by all syntactic guiles at my disposal but which will nonetheless nevertheless completely and definitively end with the trope mark we have learned to write to signal the full stop, after which is surely nothing maybe.

Form folds.
We are form and we dream it,
it nests in us like a shell,
it bases any blossoming upon our substrate for all time, it's
for the asking, had we not this
absence at our center it
would have zero affordance for its apparence, and this

is one more item in the litany of that
for which we shall have given thanks.

Into presence,
an affordance.
We rewrote it,
we encode it.
Graceful glasses,
inapparence.
Hey your optics
lost its pulses.
Ground is greyer
in empire.
There's no coda,
just the modern.
Set a tempo
by your heartbeat,
ask a neighbor,
get a key cut.

13.

Dumb fucks just do
not get the way it differs in itself,
        but Tony gets it,
Tony's an architect,
        Tony rides bikes, this
is a poem about a superhero named Tony,
        it's called "Tony's poem."

I had to set up two drinks to write this but I
                havent even taken a single sip of them yet.

No one knows the
        way to change to song, no
body knows but Hegel, &
my hair's stuck in the platen again I'm
having bad dreams but I won't bore you.

Becry a non
Yellow hay, sea deck,

Bitter here, have it, Lee,
honey knee, ooh Shema, tiff lately,
benay, I shot me hick body, likely Ma,
TV have on, Rick,
Tyvek shoe, ha ! Save, sailor.
Odd Oki he flaw, XXXX, hayseed low,
XXXX yeesh, Ma, becarry ill love,
rig so, Val ; tick harder, you !
Emery, Volvo him ; Al, miscave him ;
Window mo' , sailor.
Steve who ? Steve, hey ! To deck !
Or feet haul XXXX.
Rave, I'm homeroom, me; year, ain't it of
nestle all anal or pain echo XXXX
No tatas, Micah, believe me,
meet, take a number, tear ocean, review.
We shall own (yuck, Dave!), excavate vision,
key at a XXXX levitate, levitate,
to she way new.

I see that chance hath chosen me
 so that we talk while walking bout the rupture,
 tuning spirits in the time exchange makes in this
 summer camp or ergasterion,
but so an eyeblink shudders up the road & asks of us
how well did you prepare,
 an earthquake's just a figure for it,
where's the lit cigarette to fall & from what direction
into all this here dry brush, Smokey's changeable sign reads

FIRE DANGER VERY HIGH
but chance from where we stand is just another
name for grace, the X, that
evades iron laws, that
tells us to what limit we are free, for man stands on the threshold,
nor woman neither .

Rise and salvage our century.

For the resurrection, for
the daily resurrection, wrestling
oneself out of the corpse pose you know you have striven
all life long against this sloth, this is called
incarnation have you met it, you have, it's
half of the picture and the other half hid,
tattooed elsewhere.
For the resurrection, for
attainment of the body we shall gain for having forsaken this body,
how do we untangle doctrinal snares,
how use longing as a counterspell to cure us of our
misplaced loves.

How use longing as a counterspell
to cure us of our misplaced loves.
For what it is we were on earth

is by the resurrection proved.

For have we cleaned the heart of smut
will be legend on that day
and blazoned in us our defeat
of what it was we failed to say :

Or said we just, our flesh goes light,
the change in letters now undone,
and what greed wrought grace straight repairs,
and what was lost by us rewon.

Do you believe do you believe
and how can you believe such stuff
I know what this world thinks is wrong;
I've lived in this world long enough.

The folly of nothing is itself a picture,
Seducing you, tempting you, leading you down;
So that in the end you'll grasp for that nothing
And nothing but nothing is there to be found.

The turbid spirit met in dreams
Is us with our corrupted wish ;
The pictures that we see therein
How we have stain'd our inward eye.
For I made rot of all my wit
When with too slack a moral brace

I yoked the jade who led me wrong
And thus made tour of crummy 'hoods.

I write this here so you may know
Just what befell a one like you
When he cared not for what was right
And gave in to the spurs of lust.
What you do will haunt you ever
In your waking in your sleeping
Evenings poisoned by your longing
Yield to days regret is eating.

As man is now
the picture of himself
so in redeeméd time
the light unfoldeth so
from skin wherein is pent
that it bleeds law
pure law like food
a law without content
wherein may rest
reciting it like song
at last burden free
of body of law
of time's chast'ning spur
of any but glory
of all our predicates
and of impure prosody
so sheltered that garden

wherein we shall meet
in ruin of vestments
were mortal were poorer
and I wanna see you
my sister my spouse
o Sarah o Sara
Willn't you meet me ?

14.

Love's my tuffet,
love comes lunchtimes,
love comes to visit when I haven't a dime.
Love's for the asking,
love's a fine detour,
love is a splendid to-do with your time.
When I am mournful or
when I sit sea sick
love is the incense that staineth my air.
For one on a forcemarch to
way that all flesh goes,
gr-e-en-sle-aves was all my care.

More solid things do not
show the conplexion of the times so well
as ballads and libels.

And Flistines fought w/ Is-Ra-El
and the men of Is'rel fled
And front the mount of Gel-Bu-E
the soldiers fell down dead.

And on King Saul and on Saul's sons
Those Flistines pressed close in
And they struck down Amminadab
and lo they smote Jo-na-tan.

And Saul the king of Israel
was struck with arros, one and two,
and Saul said to his doughty page
Take thy sword and run me through.

I wont be found & I wont be mocked
by this uncircumsized band
If I must die, as die I must,
let it be by thine own hand.

From holy fear the page struck not
so Saul on his own sword fell;
and his own page then seeing Saul dead
sent himself with his sword off to hell.

The Flistines came and found the king
and hung up his corpse on a wall
Then Jabis-men came to bury the bones
And that was the end of King Saul.

Picture got by us a picture of a
hostile owning power making vigor from
the daily that it owns evil powers once were
ours mailed back to us discourteous we

groaning under weight of all we lack as tho
a vacuum open up between ourselves and
everything we could have been were world a
constitution fit to bear us, nonetheless the
words appear to mind like grace like as a
memory we thank for as we get its channels back
to antidotes of present tense hypnotic in its own
circuits of project so we rupture in the chance of
any saying breaking circuit coded by the fatal
resolution of the coming into any picture owned
in figures paid for in advance prescripted for
what we strive for in this song is just exactly
imprescriptible, a notion we shall have to come
to climax of the human actions to undertake to
give a proper meaning for, to fill it with the
plenitude of everything it seems to ask of us,
for this is what is meant when the man says
fulness of time, the paraclete now like a
satellite in nearer space, for the
word is near to you for time is near to you the
law's as close to you as your own throat.

For if it seems
that one heart split
has sought the law
but pledged the war
has went to god
in wish of grace
but acts in streets

for this world's goods
not for his gain
but to make just
the way it is
with these folks here ;
do these not twist
one to the next
so that these acts
which dont fetch grace
still yet pledge one
to've tried his hand
arriving at a covenant
such as he could
from what's down here
what ever that was
streets cash books food
words schools works tears
plans pledges patterns poems
him her me you

15.

Stumbled on a
figural fold in
how you render song,
an epoch in which pleated us
give ghosts circuits, communes, mighta-beens,
the whole unsouled panoply that poured from
engines of debt, the
Genoese strut, an instrument advowson
(vacant offices), by
such a constellation's known the way we are in time,

a picture of ourselves as figs, as
pledges, forlorn hopes, as having been walking down
the street
to the general direction of the park at some point in this life,
o city sittin' solitary,
girl I'm just gon' come and knock on your doorpost
some of these days.

Lent love
as a force
as a shift in the break,
for which we long, a

hand that guides, so that
baffled by its split decisions we're
then making pacts against these "tremors in the flesh,"
the storm from the east in the
sleeping apartments,
for to yearn's to grieve, but he
salts lights in the plackets of the earth that
just women may feat,
for let no man despair of his form he
shall be
made a woman therefore fit to be receipt of
heaven is
a scripture I read with two of my friends, while
all around us
was the business.

when we present
the patience-plays
let them take place
on the church-porch :
church porch signifieth paradice

He struts round the heap
on a rind of himself,
the last grace that of a

continued incarnation
for remission of sins,
troping the 'customed junk &
in his wits, the
reckless dead are driving now
their cars right up the mountain,
irascible as hell, and we their passengers
deducing what
deducing what
the set text reads
BE PASSERSBY.

You cannot clear the
ground but only hope, for
god selects his jurymen &
sends them yon at his good plaisir,
picking & requiting, spoiling, forgiving, for
in what shall we stand before such bar &
asking the forgiveness what we were,
how
we came to deeds such as are now so write upon our brows like
that one in the moon, the
founder of this city
us begetting the demotic

MAY, I am
able, I am
free to act, I am
allowed to. There is no
        infinitive, if
there were it would take the form mow.
        ic maeg, ic mihte, mugan, ik mag,
mahta, mega, ek ma, matti
mogen, matte, matte, mag
        mochte, magan, ik mag, mahta
to have power, to have power,
to have power, to have power

see might, see may,
        cf. the machine

16.

Then we beget our very fragile houses,
crust of issue after rains,
a tenor of the summer that is named late summer, go
out for coffee milk and for the weather,
another ambit upon rising once again from filthy crypts
to any ensemble of the particular is strapped to the
fork of its own irreversible name, and
standard issue now's the opake screw of vision piercing any
underpainted ceiling straight through to the abyss of the sky.
Answer me this, imperial largesse, where's
the heart that all the moving pictures promised me?

The creeping thing of inwit wends
a co-adjutant of the houses,
glossed and hiding in like forms
till you look up from certain angles.

Smoke's the fleet donating warp
To stable recollections of the grown
We hung our hearts up in the trees
To get to here all soaked in tone.

Nothing is
beautiful any longer this
is where we start from well
what did you expect or
rather
what do you expect, the
tyranny of any Sedgwick the
laudatory hymns of the twenty-second century TV set saying
YOU'RE MY ONE AND ONLY PRONOUN
take the money and run! ,
                                        I dreamt of you when you were
dead what did it mean I loved you a long time again & that
was now, the mind does not recognize time but it goes by
anyhow & more
                          milk is needed, milk of
you know the rest, this
             is not a prescription & I'll
not be answerable, try
                          this one on for size, you
never know until you go & I have gone to the west and bought a
pair of purple shoes there, even signed a lease or two again
my future happiness watched the tugboats drank
cider in a bag and picked out the local color alongside a
cinematographer, yes,
you won't be able to say that I didnt walk around at least
a little bit.
The name of this song's therefore : ADMONITION TO THE
AUTHOR OF
MY
EPITAPH IF I TURN OUT TO HAVE ONE.

Now stuck in
a sheltered cove
I strain to see
what works I wove.

These crimes are mine,
I must confess
done to the dead,
with no redress.

We come down here
with wound of pride
we make a mess
and then we've died.

What was the time
in which we dwelt?
It's when we stood
or when we knelt.

Standing's how we
show resistance :
kneeling tells
we need assistance.

In all of life
there's this one task :
of learning how
we ought to ask.

DAVID.

Is a signal, doesnt know
the way to get to pattern, chooses
indices that seem in some way telling, waits
for prosody not subject to external verifaction,
announces his own circular dimension & terminates
personal history for the purpose of reflection, lacks &
lacks, keeps talking but endows you with the
predicate of having chosen to be there, is only the
name a thing that is now running down on earth elected
for himself for benefit of those who are all now dead except
himself, who is certainly nathless bound to die and
wondering what if anything one ought to be doing about that,
how one ought to feel.

Wraiths cross time.

Tune the dead for real, as
 your abatement, listen in
the hollow for what resonates from
ill-lit ensembles & deposits of
they-tread-before-you, as eternal
annex to this bubble slash a form of

nudity to law not meant here as a passphrase but
<u>we're</u> <u>stricken</u> & that's where it
comes from, your despair is not my
reception, your math aint my heart,
it all goes super-slow so slow you
will be tempted towards distraction which
drags you away from the from.
The gold inside of any ache you honor with
sufficient dreaming on to it, you spill &
you lavish, you are its garment, undoing
the premises according to an upwelled sovranty in
you, accordingly it shall be known as
coronary gold. For you are washed today
for your own coronation.

17.

O weft west in a westron tried
the sort thy ilk you nath mo pail
the sort silk shock when you shot full spoil
upsiolon pent holderspoil

DINAH : As an ape I'll filch the light from your house.
STEVE : There aint no dream you could say will break me.
DINAH : May I offer : That's, like, your opinion.
STEVE : Men wake thus having thoughts to every day.
DINAH : But I'd heard our names were called by strangers.
STEVE : You know it's by our true friends wanting in.
DINAH : Say by what signs such friends of ours are known.
STEVE : That they have come before begets a trust.
DINAH : Where in your system's place for novelty?
STEVE : I dont believe in ruptured epistemes.
DINAH : But ruptured epistemes believe in you.
STEVE : Hold on a sec ; just let me send this text.
DINAH : Thou fool, thou knowst thine hast thy phone forgot!
STEVE : O shit, I must have left it at the bar.
DINAH : That's why you now cry your name in the street.
STEVE : So that with no phone my friends can find me?
DINAH : It's to insist that you still really are.
STEVE : But what(says man)'s it mean to really be?
DINAH : That's well outside the scope of our talk, Steve.

After the wedge, the law.
After the law, the current.
After the current, the shape that lingers in the current.
After the lingering, the dispersal order.
After the dispersal order, the cognitive judgment.
After the judgment, the hand-porn.
After the hand-porn, the righteous caesura.
After the caesura, the combine.
After the combine, the slipshod.
After the slipshod, the doodle.
After the doodle, the crosscheck.
After the crosscheck, the sequence of the palliatives.
After the palliatives, the L.D.S.
After the L.D.S., the ride of the valkyries.
After the valkyries, the phenomena.
After the phenomena, the question marks.
After the question marks, the voiceovers.
After the voiceovers, the last injunctions.
After the last injunctions, the lingering abstinences.
After abstinences, balance given as a halo.
After halo, time in its raw state.
After time, return to judgment, having gone round in a circle.
After the circle, ascent to the realm of the pure.
　　After ascent is the password.

Take light seriously.

To be serious means to be able to reconvene yourself ac-
cording to a new postulate, which is to find a
belt of force where it lingers undreamt of
someplace in your body. All these maneuvers can transpire in
very cramped compass, like my
heart's too strait & my house also but
a judgment enters like a draft &
flips you sideways. That's
a kind of honoring light, as I'm certain you know.
To phrase it otherwise, your particulars are
dreamt of in the other world and given substance, the
connubial bliss of the word work world's not
a mere fortuna son of man,
as the smoke ascends and you consider your votes for
  the schoolboard,
as the ambulances and the mailmen go by,
as you start to wonder when it was you failed to be
  the best observer,
what conspired against this dreaming on the part of you and
  how should you
discover means to make it open up once more, the way
  an orchid can
go for years without flowers but you manage it, you're hoping,
  hoping
takes the form of working, how long did it take you to figure that
  one out
well frankly I'm still figuring, every day I
still get out of bed

One pleas not for clemency but right,
for justice rives the body so's to send it to its fate, as
I peer through the filthy screen that
smoke and lie hath clot the
roadbed of the fortunes bred in me,
as like to strangle out the life as build a ladder via which
to get to any moon of heaven, so
I shield myself from errors by this antidote of song,
it's what we pled back, being watchmen, a-
gainst sleep, that by which we gain the crumb of knowing upon
    which we feed
in the long travail of this our supplication to a what, to what
appears to us alone in form of time & then phenomena, us
    all fumblin'
for the hem of any garment.

Speak for yourself she says I say
what do you think that means.

We carry the tent.
We meet friends.
We get going.
We talk for a while.
We find the right way.
We pass the prison.

We go over the mountain.
We sing.
We come into town.
We gather by water.
We eat the food that everybody brought.
We sing, we sing the song, we drink.
We get in the water, we
get all the way into the water.
We watch a kid, the
kid's doing a play in the water,
the kid says it all, his
mom's about had it.
You know you go out to dinner later.
To find amidst all this of what
we're made to be a manner still to
honor time.
In light of that we gathered, we
were gathered.

You write your loves down on a paper,
maybe humans choose to carry them a while,
copy them down elsewhere, that's
        the only place after a few of years where you and/or your
loves will any longer live. Strange to relate from
        how urgent life feels when you're living it but I
have met the dead and see how quick they fall from
        any human saying and that's part of the picture.

18.

MICHAEL ROW THE BOAT ASHORE // BOMBS OVER BAGHDAD

So my tutelage is stuff, the
block, the walk, the public
square, a calque for what it
would have been like in a polis with the
plenty slaves & bitches in they place,
but it is otherwise than this or is it,
not so much, Steve
Jobs that slaveowner, when comes the
jubilee of speech when we can say
as much as is within our hearts to
pour it forth, the law says yes but
the cops say no, my formal rights got
clocked in the head by your
cash in the midst of achieving the
transform, that's the lowest register of
this motet, national drone
convergence & we with right foot
pinioned to the spot by that low guile
unable therefore to tread the hill
out of this region of dissociation.
Give me your watch and I'll tell you the time,
it's just Ethiopian New Year as of this weekend,
save a seat at the table for Enoch,
he's the one who walked with the light.

I am asked of all my kin
to stand up where the law has been
and take my place among the ranks
of them that know to give god thanks.

But what has made me for this day,
and how should I know what to say?
I learned it not when I was a kid,
and thus I thought it was all hid.

I looked and looked when I was grown
in hopes of having something shown
but found only fraud and illusion
and a deepening confusion.

And now today is the first of the year
and I have learned to say that fear
of the lord is wisdom's start;
But do I know it in my heart?

I act as though I could him flee
Who every action surely sees,
as though any excuse could budge
the stern decision of the judge.

I write these verses for to show
how it is I've gone so low
and from the lowness making start
I demonstrate in humble art.

For a picture alters,
making hymns out of the law,
rhythms out of any pulse of
polis governing the change,
so that with a covenant you are charged
and all of you as well folded into time,
in order serviceable,
rolling with fortune, the
government of earth that cant be split from
providence, your choice of accent counts
you in the preterite,
passed over by the glossator, for
be my name write or be my name razed,
it falls in the scope of the judgment,

there comes a day soon,
when they will come, the
tradesmen, and burn up
all of my hair.
The wind will be like this, and
that is what the judgment looks like,
nothing but its transpiration.

You and I are together.
We can read.

The little white rabbit is eating grass.
The little bird is flying in the sky.
The foal and the little rabbit cannot fly.
Look, there is water on the ground.
There are weeds in the water.
Grass and flowers need water.
The foal and the little rabbit need water.
The little white rabbit needs to eat grass.
How many people are here?
Three people.
How many books have you got?
Five books.
We can read books.
The little boy is not sucking his finger.
How many books are there in your hands?
There are three books in my hands.
Is there water here?
The rabbit and the foal need water.

CODA

Then
I join the water.

Then, as
law, I
join the water.

Then I join the
smoke and water.

Gentle reader,
join the water.